THE RIGHTFUL POWER OF CONGRESS TO CONFISCATE AND EMANCIPATE.

"Fiat tam juris religiosissimus quam victis hostibus triumphator."
JUSTINIAN.

THE recent discussions in congress and the declamation of portions of the daily press have called the attention of the public to the questions of emancipation and confiscation. The policy of stripping the rebels of their property and liberating their slaves has been urged upon the country with much eloquence, and with an adroit appeal to the passions naturally excited by the condition of public affairs. Although the measures proposed are absolutely novel in our legislation, they are commended to the popular mind with more of rhetoric than of argument, and their constitutionality has been rather insisted on than seriously defended. But so grave a question of constitutional law cannot escape the attention of the profession, and its discussion falls strictly within the scope of a legal periodical. While its novelty and difficulty furnish a reason for its investigation, they also afford an apology for the imperfections which must always attend the discussion of a case of novel impression. In the entire absence of authority, the following pages must be regarded rather as suggestions for the solution of the question, than as an effort to arrive at any certain conclusions; and the whole purpose of this paper will have been accomplished if it shall serve to call the attention of the profession to the legal points which belong to the consideration of this topic.

At the present stage of the debates in congress, it would be idle to devote much time to any one of the many bills now pending before the two houses. As the debate has proceeded, difficulties seem to have suggested themselves to so many members, as to endanger the passage of the measure; and committees have been appointed in each house, to report bills contrived to evade the objections which have been felt, but which have not as yet been met. There are, however, certain broad principles of constitutional law which should guide the deliberations of congress, and which will govern the discussions of the courts upon this topic, in whatever form it may present itself. Most of these considerations are common to the project of confiscation and the scheme of emancipation; and it will best conduce to the brevity imposed upon this article, to discuss the two together.

There are two aspects in which these acts may be regarded. They may be considered as penal statutes, for the punishment of crime against the United States; or they may be treated as the exercise of the *jus belli* against a belligerent enemy. If we regard the rebels as citizens subject to our laws, it is obvious that they can only be deprived of their property as a punishment for some offence against the government; and congress, in legislating upon the subject, must respect the limits imposed upon its power by the constitution. If, on the other hand, we consider the rebels as enemies, liable to the treatment of belligerents in arms against the State, we are bound by the doctrines of public law, from which our belligerent rights are derived, and by which they must be limited. There is indeed no doubt that a government, in dealing with its subjects who have taken up arms against its authority, has at once the rights of a sovereign, and of a belligerent. This proposition rests upon the amplest authority. It has been laid down by the Supreme Court of the United States, in the case of *Rose* v. *Himely*, 4 Cranch, 241. See also *The Santissima Trinidad*, 7 *Wheat*, 3. It has been expressly applied to the present rebellion by Mr. Justice Dunlop, in the case of the *Tropic Wind*, which has enjoyed the unusual honors of the government press and of distribution among the foreign offices of European powers. It has been laid down by Judge Betts and Judge Cadwallader in recent prize causes argued in their respective courts, and it was affirmed by Judge Sprague in our own district in the cases of *The Revere*, and the *Amy Warwick*.

But while the government may exercise the widely different rights, springing from civil sovereignty and from the *jus belli*, it cannot do both at the same time. It may, as a belligerent, shoot down the rebels in the field, but it cannot order out a file of soldiers to execute the prisoners at Fort Warren without a trial. In dealing with each case as it arises, its action must be such as is permitted, either by the laws of the land or by the law of nations. Each act must be done either in one capacity or the other. If a citizen is to be tried for treason, he must be first indicted; if a soldier is accused of cowardice, he may be condemned by a drum-head court martial. Much of the confusion of thought, which has marked the discussion of this topic, undoubtedly proceeds from a neglect to distinguish accurately between the powers flowing from the different attitudes which the government may assume toward the rebels. From the military right of plunder, the newspapers have derived the civil penalty of confiscation. By considering the powers of the government derived from the one and the other of these sources separately, we shall be much aided in arriving at a satisfactory solution of the questions to be discussed.

I. If, then, we regard the United States as a sovereign legislating for the punishment of those who take up arms against its authority, how far may congress constitutionally provide for the confiscation of the property of the rebels and the emancipation of their slaves?

(1.) It is obvious that no new penalties can be imposed for acts already committed; for *ex post facto* laws are expressly prohibited by the constitution. It is equally plain that no law can be passed for the punishment of rebellion without providing for an inquest by a grand jury, and a trial by jury in the district where the act which forms the subject of the indictment is alleged to have been committed.—Const., Art. I., § 9. Art. of Amend., §§ 5 and 6. These are elementary propositions which hardly need mention. It may serve to illustrate the temper in which this legislation is proposed, to remark that it has been deliberately proposed in the senate to confiscate all the property of the rebels without process and without trial, and that everything should become "*ipso facto*" and at once vested in the government of the United States.

These limitations of the power of congress relate solely to the manner in which the forfeiture is to be effected. There are other difficulties inherent in the scheme itself. It is perhaps more than doubtful whether congress can pass a law affecting a convicted rebel with the entire forfeiture of his property.

(2.) The third article of the constitution, § 3, provides, "That treason shall consist only in levying war against the United States, or in adhering to their enemies giving them aid and comfort." "Congress," it proceeds, "shall have power to declare the punishment of treason; but no attainder of treason shall work corruption of blood or forfeiture except during the life of the person attainted." In construing this language, it is necessary to keep in mind the English doctrine of treason, and the well known political views of the framers of the government.

The English law of treason has always been regarded with distaste in this country. Many of the distinguished men who played a leading part in the settlement of the colonies had sought on this side of the Atlantic a freedom of thought and action which would have cost them their heads at home. The people of the colonies always sympathized with the English commonwealth, and they afforded a ready asylum to the regicides who fled from the vengeance of Charles II. These political opinions were not a little strengthened and increased by the agitation which preceded the Revolution, and by the events of the War of Independence. It is not singular that the framers of the government, themselves successful rebels, should have embodied in the constitution the popular spirit of toleration for crimes against the State.

In limiting the power of congress to legislate upon the subject of treason, they had two purposes in view. The first was to prohibit the introduction of the absurd refinements and constructions by which the statutes of treason had been converted, in the hands of pliant judges, into an engine for the suppression of reasonable political agitation; and secondly, they designed to mitigate the severities with which this crime was visited by the English law. They accordingly selected two only of the many acts which constituted treason in England, and declared that they alone should be treason against the United States, and that they should not be punished either by corruption of blood or by forfeiture beyond the life of the person attainted. This declaration must be regarded as fixing the legal nature and consequences of these acts. Having been pronounced treason by the constitution, they cannot be legislated into anything else, in such manner as to visit them with severer penalties than those named in this section. If congress may, under a new name, punish levying war in the manner in which it is forbidden to punish it as treason, this provision, which was designed to be a great constitutional bulwark, is degraded into a mere quibble about the nomenclature of criminal law; the limitation imposed upon congress becomes entirely nugatory; and the whole doctrine of allegiance, treasonable words, compassings, and constructive compassings, may flow in upon us, bringing in its train the shameless series of political plunderings which disgraced the reigns of the Stuarts.

Hence it follows that the United States, providing in its sovereign capacity for the punishment of the rebels, can only visit their crime with forfeiture for life. A controversy has however arisen regarding the extent of this prohibition. A learned writer in the North American Review insists that it applies only to forfeiture of real estate. He seems to entertain no doubt of the correctness of his opinion upon this point, for he does not hesitate to attribute to another learned writer — who deems that it includes forfeiture of personal property also — a confusion of thought upon this subject.

Yet it may not be impossible to reconcile the opinions of these eminent authorities. The writer in the North American Review is doubtless right in his position that the forfeiture prohibited in the constitution is that which was worked by an attainder by the English law. It is equally certain that this forfeiture was of real estate only. But if we consider the reason why the forfeiture was thus limited, it is by no means certain that the conclusion which he draws from these propositions is correct. By attainder, which means the entry of judgment upon a verdict of guilty of treason or of felony, the person attainted became incapable of acquiring, holding or transmitting property. Whatever belonged to him at the moment of attainder, was therefore instantly devested by it. It is however familiar learning that a person about to be attainted could in law be seised only of real property, because by the conviction preceding the attainder his personal property had already been forfeited. It is for this reason, rather than on account of any peculiarity inherent in real property, that this alone was forfeited upon attainder. If, then, we read the clause of the constitution thus, "And no attainder of treason shall work forfeiture, [such as follows an attainder by the English law, to wit, of all the property vested in the person attainted at the moment of his attainder,] except for the life of the person attainted," the difficulty is solved. This theory certainly derives some force from the reflection that both real and personal property seem to have been forfeited by attainder by act of parliament. It is entirely certain that the beneficent purpose of the constitution to punish the guilty only, and to spare the innocent, would be most imperfectly answered by reserving from forfeiture real property only.

It is also urged in behalf of the theory that real property only is exempt from forfeiture, that the doctrines of tenancy for life at common law do not apply to personal property. But although this is undoubtedly true as a general proposition, it is by no means without exception. Heir-looms are familiar to all students of English law, and the husband's rights in the wife's property furnish an obvious parallel from the civil jurisprudence. But however this may be, the argument to be drawn from the principle is not that for which it is invoked. The constitution does not say that the forfeiture upon attainder shall be for life only, but that there shall be *no* forfeiture *except* for life; and the obvious construction of this language is, that such property as by the rules of law cannot be forfeited for life shall not be forfeited at all.

(3.) We have seen that it is the well settled doctrine of our courts, that a goverment, in suppressing an insurrection, may exercise the rights of a sovereign, as well as those of a belligerent, against its rebellious subjects. Although this is undoubtedly correct as a general proposition, yet its application to the existing rebellion is to a certain extent limited and restrained by a rule of public law, familiar to our own tribunals, and older than the reign of Henry VII. in England.

It is unhappily an incontrovertible fact that the authority of the government has ceased to operate throughout a large district of the Republic. The coast of this territory has been subjected to a blockade notified according to the law of nations, and enforced in the manner prescribed by that code. Commercial and personal intercourse between the loyal States and the insurgent country has been prohibited by the government, and the transportation of the mails has ceased. The process of the United States cannot be executed, and throughout the entire region occupied by the rebels, no person exercises authority under a commission from the United States. For the time being, the government has ceased to govern within the rebellious district, and is powerless to afford to its citizens that protection and assistance which is the great end of its existence and the just source of its authority. These results have been accomplished against the consent of the government, and in spite of its strenuous effort, and are undertaken and maintained by the force of arms.

It is a well settled proposition of public law, that such an exclusion of a government from its territory by a public enemy suspends the operation of its laws, and temporarily releases the inhabitants of the occupied district from their allegiance. In the war of 1812, the occupation of the port of Castine by the British gave rise to causes in which this doctrine was discussed in the courts of the United States. During the period while that town was held by the British, various importations of goods from the British Colonies were made by the American merchants, in violation of the non-intercourse acts. After the withdrawal of the enemy's forces an attempt was made to enforce the penalties imposed by these statutes; but the Circuit Court of the United States held that the obligation of obedience to them was suspended by the military occupation of the place; and this doctrine was afterwards affirmed by the Supreme Court of the United States. *U. S.* v. *Hayward*, 2 *Gallis.* 485; *U. S.* v. *Rice*, 4 *Wheat.* 246.

In the latter case, Mr. Justice Story, in delivering the opinion of the court, said, "By the conquest and military occupation of Castine, the enemy acquired that firm possession which enabled him to exercise the fullest rights of sovereignty over that place. The sovereignty of the United States was suspended, and the laws of the United States could no longer be rightfully enforced there, or be obligatory upon the inhabitants who remained and submitted to the conquerors. By the surrender the inhabitants passed under a temporary allegiance to the British government, and were bound by such laws, and such only, as it chose to recognize and impose. From the nature of the case no other laws could be obligatory upon them; for where there is no protection, or allegiance, or sovereignty, there can be no claim to obedience."

This doctrine derives especial force in its application to the condition of public affairs growing out of the rebellion from the fact that the laws, thus declared to be inoperative, were not ordinary acts for the regulation of commerce, but were hostile measures designed to injure the enemy. At that period it was the universal practice of belligerents to wage war against the enemy's commerce, and the system of embargoes and blockades was esteemed one of the most efficient engines of warfare. In violating the non-intercourse acts, and trading with the British Colonies, the citizens of Castine were, according to the theories of that period, giving aid and comfort to the enemy.

It will be observed that in *United States* v. *Rice*, the court put the suspension of the obligation of obedience distinctly on the ground that the government had ceased to govern and protect its citizens. It is manifest that the doctrine could not be derived from any rights of conquest acquired by the British; for conquest only becomes complete by recognition by treaty, or by the abandonment of all effort to regain the occupied district. In *United States* v. *Hayward*, this distinction is taken by Judge Story: "It could not," he says, "strictly speaking, be deemed a port within the dominions of Great Britain, for it had not permanently passed under her sovereignty. The right which existed was the mere right of superior force." In *Fleming* v. *Page*, 9 How. 614, it was held that Tampico, which was occupied by our troops during the Mexican war, did not thereby become a part of the United States. See also *Cross* v. *Harrison*, 16 How. 164. It is thus apparent that it is the exclusion of the old government from the place occupied, and not its incorporation into the hostile state, by which the citizen is released from the obligation of obedience. When a government is no longer able to govern and protect its citizens, it has no right to demand that they should obey its laws.

If the doctrine of these cases be sound—and many English authorities might be cited to this point—it seems that congress cannot legislate in such manner as to bind those persons who are within the district from which our authority is excluded by the rebels. It is not doubted that there is a distinction between an occupation by a recognized power, and the exclusion of the rightful authority by organized rebellion. But that distinction does not appear to touch this doctrine, which flows purely from the fact of military occupation. The force excluding the legitimate government does not derive any authority from the laws and institutions of the government which it serves. The citizen of the occupied place does not justify his disobedience on the ground that he is the subject of another power. He rests his case solely on the broad ground that his own government, having been driven away, and being no longer able to protect and govern him, cannot during its absence lay rightful claim to his obedience. So far as this is the case in the Southern States, it is difficult to see why the same result must not flow from the same state of facts.

(4.) Many persons who will concede the application of this doctrine to the non-combatant inhabitants of the Southern States, will deny that it embraces the case of those who are in arms against the authority of the government. There can be no doubt that those who were concerned in the commencement of the rebellion are liable to the penalties of the acts which they transgressed. Should it be found practicable to make the distinction, those who, as chiefs and leaders, are engaged in effecting the exclusion of the authority of the government from the South, may perhaps be answerable for all their acts tending to that result. But that is not the question now before us. The inquiry now under consideration is, whether, while our authority is wholly excluded from a given territory, we can pass laws to visit with penalties acts done within that district pending such exclusion. Has congress the rightful power to legislate to punish acts done in obedience to those authorities who afford to the rebels those advantages of a government which we ourselves cannot at present give them? Whatever may be our wishes and our prejudices upon this point, it would seem upon authority that it has not. The masses in arms against the authority of the United States, and those who by their labor are aiding them in their military operations, are, by the English law of treason, not liable to punishment so long as the rebellion preserves the form and consistency which has heretofore marked its history.

It is laid down in the preamble of the Stat. of 11th Henry VII., that "The subjects of England are bound by the duty of their allegiance to serve their prince and sovereign *for the time being*, in defence of him and his realm against every rebellion, power, and might raised against him; and that whatsoever may happen against the mind and will of the prince, as in this land some time past it hath been seen, it is not reasonable, but against all laws, reason, and good conscience, that such subjects attending upon such service should suffer for doing their true duty and service of allegiance." It is then enacted that no person attending upon the king for the time being in his wars, shall, for such service, be convict or attaint of treason or other offence by act of parliament, or otherwise by any process of law. This statute, which was passed at the conclusion of the Wars of the Roses, relates to those who bear arms in behalf of the king in possession—even against him who claims by right of inheritance. It is said by Sir Michael Foster, that this is a clear and full parliamentary declaration of the ancient law and constitution of England. "This putteth the duty of the subject upon a rational and safe bottom. He knoweth that protection and allegiance are reciprocal duties." "He seeth the fountain from whence the blessings of a government, liberty, peace, and plenty flow to him, and there he payeth his allegiance."—*Foster*, *Crown Law*, 399. Lord Coke lays down the same rule, and says that this does not mean the king who has been crowned and is in possession of the insignia of royalty, "for coronation is but an ornament or solemnity of honor." In his reading in the statute 25 E., 3 *De Proditionibus*, he says: "This act is to be understood of a king in possession of the crowne and kingdom; for if a king regnant in possession, although he be *rex de facto et non de jure*, yet is he Seignior le Roy within the purvieu of this statute. And the other, which hath right, and is out of possession, is not within this act." 3 *Inst.* 7.

It is true that this constitutional principle has been sometimes violated in England. It was distinctly disregarded in the case of Sir Henry Vane, whose trial and execution have been held by all liberal writers to have been disgraceful to his judges and to the king. Hallam speaks of it as "one of the most reprehensible acts of that bad reign." Even those who defend the conviction rather apologize for than sustain it, and its advocates have not been able to agree upon the ground on which it is to be upheld. Serjeant Hawkins seems to be of opinion that it may be maintained on the distinction that, while Cromwell was in possession of the kingdom, he yet was not king, and "thus that no other person" than Charles II. "was in possession of any sovereign power known to our [English] law." *Bk.* 1, *c.* 2, § 18. With this agrees Lord Chief Baron Bridgman's construction of the Statute of Henry VII., in the trial of *John Cook, the Regicide*—"That King Henry VII. did was to take care of the king *de facto* against the king *de jure;* it was for a king and a kingly government, it was not for an anti-monarchical government." 5 *State Trials*, 1114. It appears by the report of the trial, that Sir Henry Vane's judges got over the difficulty by resolving that Charles II. was king both *de jure* and *de facto*. They refused to hear argument upon the point, and stopped Sir Henry with the remark that they would not admit that the king was ever out of possession.

A case thus scandalously conducted cannot be considered of any weight upon this point of constitutional law. It has been steadily denied by those lawyers who have combated the royal prerogative in England, and there has been but one opinion in regard to it upon this side of the Atlantic. It would be somewhat of a novelty to see the doctrines of Sir Henry Vane's case adopted and maintained by the descendants of the inhabitants of the Colony of Massachusetts Bay.

The sound constitutional principle which is the result of the authorities seems to be this: Where a usurping power has seized upon the government and excluded the rightful authority for the exercise of its functions, it may claim the obedience of the district throughout which its power extends. If, in obedience to the command of this power, the inhabitants take up arms against their lawful sovereign, they are not liable to the pains and penalties of treason. The power which actually governs may be safely served in arms by those whom it protects.

But while this principle is easily deduced from the authorities, the limits of its application are obscure and doubtful. It is difficult to lay down rules for determining when the citizen may safely obey the usurper against his rightful sovereign; and it is nearly impossible to ascertain at what stage of the downfall of the rebel government this justification will cease to be valid. But to assert that the government may legislate for the punishment of acts done within a district where it has wholly ceased to exercise authority, is to deny the whole doctrine, and to fall back upon the high Tory theories, which have until now found no defenders among American jurists.

There are doubtless many persons to whom these doctrines will prove distateful. It is only natural that those who are moved by their passions should resent the limits imposed upon them by the laws. But it is for this purpose that constitutions are made, and the principles which they consecrate will be worthless, if they are to bend before the blast of popular fury. It would be vain to argue with those who refuse to recognize the binding force of constitutional prohibition, in dealing with the rebels. It is believed, however, that such is not the temper of the people, and it certainly cannot be the spirit of the profession, who remember the rule laid down in *Calvin's case:* "*Optima regula, qua nulla est verior aut firmior in jure, neminem oportet esse sapientiorem legibus.*" 7 Co. 1. The rule of law for which we contend, applied to the case of this rebellion, will work out a result which all will agree to be just and reasonable. The conspirators who inaugurated the rebellion will pay the penalties of their crime; their misled followers who have submitted to their usurpations are not liable to that punishment, which it would be inconsistent with the practice of civilized nations, and with the dictates of humanity, to inflict upon them.

II. We have already seen that the United States, in addition to its rights as a sovereign, may exercise against the rebels the rights flowing from the *jus belli.* The event of a rebellion is provided for by the clause of the constitution conferring upon congress the power to "provide for calling out the militia to execute the laws of the Union, suppress insurrections, and repel invasions;" and there can be no doubt that, in employing the force of the United States, their commander-in-chief may rightfully do with them whatever the laws of war permit a belligerent to do against an enemy. It therefore remains for us to inquire how far the law of nations which regulates the exercise of hostilities, recognizes confiscation and emancipation among the legitimate acts of warfare. There can be no doubt that the rules of war among civilized nations are binding upon congress, and it cannot be presumed that it would wilfully violate them in its legislation. The just fame which the United States have acquired in their efforts to soften and ameliorate the code of war, forbids that they should seek to exercise those rights, the legality of which they have steadily denied.

(1.) Whatever may have been the ancient rule in regard to the treatment of enemies in war, it has long been settled by the usage of civilized nations, that hostilities must be conducted within certain established limits. As long ago as the days of the Roman Republic this doctrine was recognized by Fabricius in his celebrated reply to the proposition made to him to poison King Pyrrhus. "*Non fraude nec occulte, sed palam et armatum populum Romanum hostes suos ulcisci.*" The person of the enemy has long been protected against all harm except such as may be necessarily inflicted in battle. In regard to property, the rule, if more recently recognized, is no longer doubtful. It is conceded, that unless in exceptional cases, the private property of enemy's subjects upon land is not liable to seizure; and that even the right of conquest includes the confiscation of the public property only of the conquered State. Nor can any distinction be accurately taken between a rebellion and a public war in the application of this rule; for it is settled by the concurrent authority of all writers on International Law, that in all wars, each subject of the contending parties is involved in hostilities equally with the State itself. *Halleck*, 425; *Wheaton*, 419.

This distinction between the confiscation of public and private property in war is now firmly established in the law of nations. It may indeed be doubted whether the entire property of the subjects of the enemy has ever been confiscated since the days of the Roman Republic. Wheaton says that the last instance of the universal confiscation of real property occurred at the conquest of England by William the Conquerer.—*Elements*, p. 420. All respectable writers of modern times agree in exempting private property on land from confiscation.—*Heffter*, § 133; *Halleck*, 457; *Wheaton's Elements*, 420. Isambert, a distinguished French writer on International Law, lays down the rule as follows: "Nous pensons avec Grotius qu'on acquiert par une guerre juste autant de choses qu'il en faut pour indemniser completement les frais de la guerre; mais il n'est pas vrai que par le droit des gens on acquiert le droit de la propriété entière des biens des sujets." *Annales Politiques et Diplomat.*, *Introduction* (*Par.* 1823), p. 115. *Zacharia* 40, *B. von Staate* iv. p. 102, is yet more distinct upon this question: "The private property of enemy's subjects is under the protection of the Law of Nations; it is only liable to seizure in exceptional cases, and where circumstances render the purpose of the war unattainable in any other way." In *U. S.* v. *Percheman*, 7 Peters, 51, Chief Justice Marshall, in speaking of conquest, says: "The modern usage of nations which has become law would be violated, that sense of justice and of right which is acknowledged and felt by the whole civilized world would be outraged, if private property should be generally confiscated, and private rights annulled."

The case of *Brown* v. *United States*, 8 Cranch, has been relied upon as an authority for the proposition that by the law of nations, as recognized in this country, the right of confiscating enemy's property belongs to a belligerent. It will be found upon examination that no such question arose in that case. The point there decided was, that enemy's property in the country does not become liable to be libelled as prize by the mere declaration of war. It is true that the courts go farther, and say that congress has power to confiscate such property if it see fit to do so. But it must be observed, that this remark was not necessary to the decision of the case. It is unquestionably true that there is no constitutional prohibition upon such legislation; but the obligation imposed by the Law of Nations is none the less binding upon that account, and the United States could hardly satisfy the reproaches of civilized powers for an infringement of that code, by the plea that it was not unconstitutional. Against this *dictum* of Chief Justice Marshall in 1814, we may well set the *dictum* of the same great magistrate in *United States* v. *Percheman*, nearly twenty years later, and at a time when the United States had publicly and conspicuously embraced its doctrine.

There is indeed no doubt that the United States is thoroughly committed to the doctrine that enemy's private property on land is not lawful prize of war. It has been repeatedly asserted by the State department in the diplomatic intercourse of the country. Before the adoption of the constitution, it was denied in the debates of the congress of the Confederation, that a capture and possession by the enemy of movable property extinguished or affected the title of the owners. In the *Madison Papers*, six States appear to have given their adhesion to this proposition. 5 *Elliot's Debates*, 16. One of the earliest acts of the government was an effort to abolish privateering, which was put upon the express ground that private property on land was exempt from capture, and that the same rule ought to apply to maritime captures also. In 1823, John Quincy Adams, then secretary of state, held the following language upon this subject in his instructions to Mr. Rush, at London: "By the usage of nations the private property of an enemy is protected from seizure and confiscation as such." "By an exception, the reason of which it is not easy to perceive, the private property of an enemy has not received the benefit of the same principle." Such also was the position assumed by Mr. Marcy in his celebrated letter to Count Sartiges, relating to the propositions of public law laid down by the Congress of Paris.

But the most important and conspicuous assertion of this doctrine by the United States occurred in the discussion with Great Britain, which grew out of the first article of the Treaty of Ghent. It was stipulated by that article that all places, taken by either party, should be restored without delay, without carrying away public property captured in such place, or any slaves or other private property. 8 *U. S. Sts. at Large*, 214. Notwithstanding this stipulation, the British, upon the evacuation, removed a number of negroes who had been captured in predatory expeditions, or who had voluntarily taken refuge beneath their flag. It was claimed by the United States that this was not only an open violation of the stipulation of the treaty, but also that it was against the laws of civilized warfare. John Quincy Adams, then minister at the Court of St. James, was charged with the negotiation on the part of the United States. In his letter to the secretary of state, dated August 22d, 1815, he narrates his conversation with Lord Castlereagh upon this subject, a portion of which is as follows: "Had the British plenipotentiaries asked of us an explanation of our proposal to transpose the words [of the treaty,] we should certainly have given it: we evidently had an object in making the proposal; and we thought the words themselves fully disclosed it. Our object was the restoration of all property which, by the usages of war among civilized nations, ought not to have been taken. All private property on shore was of that description; it was entitled by the laws of war to exemption from capture, — slaves were private property." Further on he continues: "It was true, proclamations inviting slaves to desert from their masters had been issued by British officers; we believe them deviations from the usages of war; we believed that the British government itself would, when the hostile passions arising from the state of war should subside, consider them in the same light. * * * Lord Liverpool manifested no dissatisfaction at these remarks, nor did he attempt to justify the proclamation to which I particularly alluded." *Amer. State Papers*, xi. 211.

The result of this diplomatic discussion was an agreement to leave the matter in controversy to the arbitration of the Emperor of Russia. Before the cause was argued, Mr. Munroe had become president, and had appointed Mr. Adams his secretary of state. In this capacity it became his duty to prepare the instructions to Mr. Middleton, to whom, as minister at St. Petersburg, the argument in our behalf was entrusted. On the 5th of July, 1820, he addressed to that gentleman an elaborate despatch, in which the position assumed by our government is set forth at great length. After speaking of the agreement in regard to public property, he proceeds as follows:

"But private property was not, and could not be, lawfully taken with the place. With the exception of maritime captures, private property in captured places is by the laws of nations respected — none could lawfully be taken — and the stipulation was that none should be carried away. * * * The British nation as well as the United States consider slaves as property — slaves belonging to private individuals as private property; millions of such slaves are held as property in the British dominions, and they are recognized as such by the terms of the article. * * *

"It has been repeatedly alleged on the part of the British government, that it could not be supposed they would have agreed to an article which would oblige them to deliver up to their masters slaves who, during the war, had taken refuge under their protection. The reply to this observation is, that if that had been an objection to their agreeing to the article, it should have been made before the signing of the article, and the engagement not to carry away slaves at all. They had in fact numbers of slaves by these different modes of capture, — one of such as had been seduced to run away from their masters by proclamations from British officers; a second of voluntary fugitives whom they received; and a third of such as had been taken in predatory excursions. You will find in Niles' Register, vol. vi. p. 242, the proclamation of Admiral Cochrane, instigating the desertion of slaves from their masters. * * * It is not openly addressed to slaves, nor does it avow its real object. From the use of the phraseology which it adopts, the inference is conclusive that the real object was such as the admiral did not choose to avow, and the only supposable motive for the disguise is the consciousness that it was not conformable to the established usages of war among civilized nations. The wrong was in the proclamation. *Admiral Cochrane had no lawful authority to give freedom to the slaves belonging to the citizens of the United States. The recognition of them by Great Britain in the treaty as property, is a complete disclaimer of the right to destroy that property by making them free.* Any engagement contracted with them to that effect was, in relation to the owners of the property, wrongful; and, if, in relation to the slaves themselves, it was an engagement which the British government assumed upon themselves and sanctioned, it could not divest the owners of the slaves of their property, nor release the British government from the obligation to the United States, and to the owners, to evacuate the place without carrying them away."

On the 7th of July, 1820, he wrote to Mr. Rush, who was still at London: "The only equity of the British side is that they signed the article without being aware of its full import, and that the stipulation was incompatible with their previous promises to the negroes. This is the real knot of the question between us, and its solution is that they had no right to make any such promises to the negroes. The principle is, *that the emancipation of enemy's slaves is not among the acts of legitimate war* — as relates to the owners, it is a destruction of private property, nowhere warranted by the usages of war. This principle must, I think, be peculiarly familiar to the Emperor of Russia, and may be pressed upon his attention in the case of reference with effect."

On the 18th of October, 1820, he again wrote to Mr. Middleton: "In the statement of the British ground of argument upon the claim in the submission, they have broadly asserted the right of emancipating slaves — private property — as a legitimate right of war. This is utterly incomprehensible on the part of a nation whose subjects hold slaves by millions, and who, in this very treaty, recognize them as private property. No such right is acknowledged as a law of war by writers who admit *any* limitation. The right of putting to death all prisoners in cold blood and without special cause, might as well be pretended to be a law of war, or the right to use poisoned weapons, or to assassinate. I think the emperor will not recognize the right of emancipation a legitimate warfare, and am persuaded you will present the argument against it. * * * "[1]

The result of this discussion was a decision in favor of the United States, based, however, upon the language of the treaty. The emperor declined to pass upon the other ques-

---

[1] The portions italicised in these extracts are underscored in the original. The writer is under much obligation to John Quincy Adams, Esq., for his kindness in permitting him to have access to the papers of his distinguished grandfather, and to copy from them the portions printed in the text. It is believed that the despatch from which they are taken has never been given to the public.

tions argued between the parties, on the ground that they did not arise upon the submission.

By these extracts it will be seen that the government of the United States is publicly pledged to two propositions of public law:

1st. That the property of private persons is not liable to seizure and confiscation in war.

2d. That in waging war against a slaveholding nation, the slaves of private persons are to be treated as private property, and that it is not within the limits of legitimate hostilities to capture or entice them from their masters.

To these propositions the United States are committed. They cannot deny them, without rendering themselves justly liable to the reproach of asserting in their own behalf a doctrine which they refuse to apply to others. A nation cannot honorably practice against an enemy that method of warfare which it denounces as illegitimate, when employed against itself. It would be better to submit to difficulty and danger than to sully the pages of our history with the record of duplicity and unfairness.

These propositions are not only binding upon the honor of the country; but they are commended to the reason of the student by the great authority to which the opinions of Mr. Adams upon questions of public law are justly entitled. Few American diplomatists have been so profoundly versed in public law, and none have excelled him in uprightness and in sense of national honor. His well-known love of freedom renders it certain that his views in regard to the slave question were not influenced by passion or prejudice. If at a later period of his life, amid the excitements of a heated and personal debate, he expressed opinions somewhat at variance with those of his diplomatic argument of this question, it should not be forgotten that in this instance he was speaking with all the responsibility of a minister of state, while in that he was defending himself against a parliamentary attack of unexampled bitterness.

(2.) If the government is prepared to repudiate a doctrine to which it is thus solemnly committed, the question is by no means exhausted. There is a broad distinction recognized by the law of nations, between the capture of real and of personal property. All jurists are agreed that the right of capture can only be exercised by taking possession of the enemy's property. Paper decrees and proclamations are wholly ineffectual to devest property. So far as personal chattels on land are concerned, the captor acquires an absolute title to them, when he has taken them into his custody, and removed them into a place of safety. The essence of this title is possession, and without it nothing is acquired. If therefore it is proposed to confiscate all chattels of rebels, it is necessary that they should be seized and securely held by the military power. *Halleck*, 447. *Heffter*, § 130. *Wheaton Elements*, 436.

In regard to real property the case is otherwise. The possession of this does not pass the title to the enemy occupying it, but merely confers the right to use and enjoy it so long as the occupation continues. Possession does not ripen into title until it has been confirmed either by a conquest recognized by treaty, or conceded by an abandonment of all effort to regain the occupied territory. *Halleck*, 447; *Heffter*, § 131. If the captor alienates pending the occupation, and the territory is afterward recovered or restored, the new tenant has no title against the former owner. *Halleck*, 449; *Heffter*, § 133. Hence it is apparent that by the rules which govern the relations of belligerents to each other the confiscation of the real property of the rebels is impossible. The hostilities now conducted by the United States cannot result in conquest, for there is nothing to conquer. The *de facto* power, which has excluded the United States from their rightful jurisdiction, holds its territory solely by a naked possession, from which no rights can be derived. When that power shall be conquered, it will cease to exist, and the government will resume its ancient rights. It will exercise the authority derived from the constitution, not the *jus victoriæ*, the right of conquest.

The history of the origin and progress of the rebellion establishes the proposition upon an impregnable basis. The power exercised by the government of the United States, in carrying on hostilities against the rebels, is the constitutional function of suppressing an insurrection. This is everywhere stated in the proclamations of the President, and in the acts of congress passed at the session in July, 1861; and the voluminous diplomatic correspondence of Secretary Seward is chiefly devoted to enforcing this proposition upon the European powers. It is for the purpose of suppressing this insurrection that our armies are in the field. The President's proclamation of April 15th, 1861, calls out the militia "to suppress said combinations, and to cause the laws to be fully executed." "The utmost care," he says, "will be observed, consistently with the object aforesaid, to avoid any devastations, any destruction of or any interference with property, or any disturbance of peaceful citizens in any part of the country." In the proclamation of May 5th, 1861, the President invokes the co-operation of all good citizens in the measures thereby adopted for the effectual suppression of unlawful violence, for the impartial enforcement of constitutional laws, and for the speediest possible restoration of peace and order, and, with them, of happiness and prosperity throughout the country.

The theory of this legislative and executive action, that the rights of conquest do not grow out of the suppression of an insurrection, seems to have been the doctrine of ancient Rome. The rule of the civil law upon this subject is laid down in l. 21, § 1, *D. de captiv.* as follows: "*In civilibus dissensionibus quamvis semper per eas respublica lædatur, non tamen in exitium reipublicæ contenditur; qui in alterutras partes discedent, vice hostium non sunt eorum inter quos jura captivitatum aut postliminiorum fuerint, et ideo captos et venundatos, posteaque manumissos placuit, supervacuo repetere a Principe ingenuitatem quam nulla captivitate amiserant.*" Although this proposition relates only to the person of the captured rebel, it applies equally to his property, for by the rule of the civil law they were regarded alike. The best title known to that system was that gained by capture. "*Omnium maxime sua esse credebant quæ ex hostibus cepissent.*" *Gaius* iv. 16. In civil wars, however, the rule did not apply, and the sole prize of the victor was the restoration of the authority of the State.

(3.) If we admit the right to confiscate such property of the enemy as may be seized by the military power, it does not follow that universal confiscation is permitted by the law of nations. The extent of that right obviously admits of no definition, for its exercise is determined by the will of the victor. But it can hardly be doubted that it does not justify the complete spoliation of an entire people. There is no instance in modern history in which a conqueror, however victorious, has attempted to seize the whole property of the subjects of the conquered State. Napoleon, no gentle victor, confined himself to the imposition of pecuniary subsidies, and to the levy of commissary stores for his troops. The United States, completely victorious in Mexico, carefully refrained from touching the private property of the Mexicans, and looked to the State alone for indemnity and security. It is impossible to claim as a recognized belligerent right, a power which no belligerent has exercised in modern times. And although it may be difficult to fix the just limits to the right of the victor, it will be conceded that they cannot be carried to an extent unknown in civilized warfare.

(4.) We have thus seen that the right of confiscation derived from the *jus belli*, if it exists at all, relates only to such personal property as may be seized by the military power, while real property is only liable to temporary occupation during the existence of hostilities. It only remains to inquire by whom this right, thus limited, may be exercised.

It is plain that congress has no power to legislate in regard to the operations of the army in the field. It cannot prescribe by statute a plan of campaign, or pass laws to regulate the manœuvres of the troops. These matters evidently belong to the President as commander-in-chief of the forces, and are to be determined by him according to the dictates of his military judgment. It will not be contended that a law, requiring the assault upon a besieged town to be undertaken within a certain number of hours after the investment, would be within the scope of the constitutional power of congress; and it is perhaps equally apparent that congress cannot fix by statute the terms to be granted to the garrison of a besieged place, for this must depend upon military consideration, and the condition of the investing force must often govern the determination of the question. The treatment of the inhabitants of a district under military occupation is often an important element in the success of a campaign. A striking instance of this truth is afforded by a case which arose in the Mexican war. The President issued an order to General Scott, commanding him to levy contributions for the subsistence of his army upon the region occupied by our troops. To this order the General replied by the following energetic remonstrance: "If it be expected at Washington * * * that this army is to support itself by forced contributions levied upon the country, we may ruin and exasperate the inhabitants and starve ourselves; for it is certain that they would sooner remove or destroy the products of their farms, than allow them to fall into our hands without compensation. Not a ration for man or horse would be brought in except by the bayonet, which would oblige the troops to spread themselves out many leagues to the right and left, and to stop all military operations."—*Scott to Marcy*, May 20th, 1847. In accordance with the views of this protest, the General disobeyed the order of the President; and Gen. Halleck tells us, in his excellent work on military science, that this course was attended with the happiest results.

It can hardly be doubted that in cases where the exercise

of the military right of capturing enemy's property is thus vitally connected with the prosecution of the campaign, it would be an improper interference with the functions of the executive to attempt to direct it by legislation. Yet it is obvious that the occasions when such would be the case, cannot be foreseen. A law requiring the general commanding a *corps d'armée* to seize all rebel property, or to emancipate slaves as he advanced, could hardly fail to exercise an influence on the operations of the campaign; and if no discretion is left him, it is difficult to understand how congress can legislate upon the subject, without meddling unduly and dangerously with the functions of the commander-in-chief, and of those entrusted by him with the command of the armies of the United States.

If we examine the constitution itself, no clause will be found conferring upon congress the power to legislate upon this subject. In the theory of the distribution of the powers of the government, it belongs to the legislature to raise and support armies, to make rules for their government, and to declare war. It is then for the executive to conduct the hostilities to a successful end, and to make the treaty of peace. It is also provided that congress may make rules concerning captures on land and water. These are all the provisions which confer power to legislate in regard to matters belonging to the military establishment and operations of the United States. By none of them does the power to confiscate, or to require commanding generals to confiscate, appear to be granted.

A comparison of the language conferring the power "to make rules for the government and regulation of the land and naval forces," with the same clause in the articles of confederation, will show that this clause of the constitution relates only to the internal government and police of the troops, and not to the direction of their operations in the field. By the articles of confederation, congress had the power "of making rules for the government and regulation of said land and naval forces, and directing their operations." The former part of this language plainly relates to the internal government, and the latter to the command of the forces in the field. And it will be conceded that where a clause of the articles of confederation, having a settled meaning, is incorporated into the constitution, it must bear there the same construction.

In the Confederation, both of these powers were conferred upon congress, which exercised both executive and legislative functions. By the constitution the language conferring the power of internal government of the forces is retained, but the clause concerning the "direction of the operations" disappears. It is probable that this change resulted from the distribution of the power of the government, and that this omission was caused by the intended transfer of the power to the commander-in-chief.

It has already been stated that Chief Justice Marshall, in delivering the opinion of the court in *Brown* v. *The United States*, cited above, laid down the *dictum* that congress, under the power to make rules concerning captures, may confiscate enemy's property found within the United States at the time of the declaration of war. The importance of this *dictum* cannot be denied. But it is also true that there are grave arguments against its doctrine, which were not presented at the hearing of that cause, which might perhaps have affected the opinion of the chief justice; and it should not be overlooked that the confiscation spoken of in this *dictum* affects property already within the jurisdiction of the United States, and does not at all relate to enemy's property on enemy's soil.

The clause of the constitution upon which this *dictum* is based, is, like the one just considered, derived from the articles of confederation, where it reads as follows: "Congress shall have the power of establishing rules for deciding in all cases what captures on land or water shall be legal, and in what manner the prizes taken on land or water shall be divided or appropriated." Two powers are included in this grant; first, the power to decide what captures shall be legally made; and secondly, how the property captured pursuant to law shall be disposed of. Under the former, congress could direct the capture of whatever it might deem fit; while by the latter, the power is conferred to regulate the distribution and apportionment of prize.

In the constitution, this clause is materially changed. No mention is made of the first power granted to the congress of the confederation, and the latter appears in a more condensed form. The language of the clause seems to relate rather to captures when made, than to the act of making them. This has been the uniform construction given to it by congress. The prize act, passed on July 26th, 1812, while providing minutely for the disposition of captured property, does not attempt to determine what shall be captured. In like manner the army and navy acts contain only provisions for the disposal of the booty and prize made by the respective forces. In the Mexican war no legislation was had upon the subject.

The change made in the language of the clause of the constitution relating to this subject, from the language of the articles of confederation, seems to be best accounted for by the supposition that it was the design of the framers of the government to confer upon the commander-in-chief the power to decide what captures should be made. So long as the congress was the sole governing body, this power necessarily belonged to its sphere of action; but the creation of an executive department, probably led to its omission among the powers of congress, in obedience to the theory that it belonged more appropriately to the military functions conferred upon the President.

It is not contended that this reasoning is conclusive in regard to the power of congress to legislate upon this question. In the entire absence of authority it would be presumptuous to attempt to lay down a certain rule. It is not however too much to claim that the existence of the power is at least doubtful, and that its attempted exercise may establish a precedent capable of giving rise to serious difficulties in future wars. It was a familiar maxim of the first Napoleon, that one bad general is better than two good ones, to command an army. The correspondence of Washington bears testimony to the mischiefs which result from the power of a legislative body to interfere with military operations in the field, and there is certainly nothing in the recent experience of the country to encourage the assumption by civilians of the power to affect or control the management of a campaign.

If the propositions laid down in these pages are correct, it appears that the rightful power of congress to confiscate and emancipate is limited by the Constitution of the United States, and by the laws of war as recognized by civilized nations. In dealing with the rebels as a sovereign, the United States can only confiscate their property as a penalty for the crime of which they are guilty, which is defined by the constitution to be treason. It must afford to each person accused of this crime, a trial by jury in the State and district where the offence is committed, which trial must be upon a presentment by a grand jury. Congress may declare the punishment of treason, but this can only extend to the forfeiture of a life estate in the property of the person attainted. It cannot be doubted that this is the rule in relation to real estate, and there is reason to hold that it includes personal property also. And finally it may be doubted whether those persons who have taken up arms against the government, since its authority has been forcibly excluded from the territory occupied by the rebellion, can be made liable for acts done during the period of such exclusion.

As a belligerent, the United States may do to the rebels whatever the laws of war permit against an enemy. The government has however constantly claimed, in its diplomatic intercourse with foreign powers, that by the laws of nations private property is exempt from confiscation. By the position assumed by the State Department, in the arbitration growing out of the Treaty of Ghent, it seem to be publicly committed to the doctrine that the seizure or enticing away of enemy's slaves is not a legitimate act of warfare. If these doctrines are repudiated, it is certain that the personal property of the rebels is alone liable to confiscation; for the rights of complete conquest, by which alone an enemy can be divested of his real property, cannot be acquired in civil wars. The belligerent right of confiscation can be exercised only by manucaption; and such personal property as escapes seizure is not affected by any decrees or proclamations. And it may well be doubted whether congress has any power to legislate in regard to the exercise of this military right, which, by the spirit and the terms of the constitution, seems to belong to the commander-in-chief of the armies of the United States.

It is not expected that these conclusions will command universal assent. "To what lengths," says Sir Michael Foster, "cannot the sweets of revenge, the joys of conquest, the prospect of rich plunder in a plenty of confiscations, with a misgiving heart still dreading the final issue of things—to what lengths of violence cannot these incitements carry the vindictive, the ravenous, the timid blustering mortals, who upon such revolutions either take the lead or join in the cry. At such times as these the still voice of law and reason is seldom heard."

www.ingramcontent.com/pod-product-compliance
Lightning Source LLC
LaVergne TN
LVHW011142110826
845150LV00008B/2466

* 9 7 8 1 4 1 8 1 9 3 3 6 2 *